Series 606A

STORIES IN THIS BOOK

Saint George

Saint Andrew

Saint David

Saint Patrick

Saint Francis of Assisi

Saint Christopher

Saint Margaret of Scotland

Saint Joan of Arc

A LADYBIRD 'EASY-READING' BOOK

A First Book of
SAINTS

by HILDA I. ROSTRON
with illustrations by
MARTIN AITCHISON

Ladybird Books Ltd Loughborough

SAINT GEORGE

Saint George is the patron saint of England. The father of George was a nobleman who served in the Roman army.

As the son of a soldier, George grew up knowing what it was to be brave. He, too, became a soldier and well-known for his bravery.

The Emperor of Rome had made a law that Christians must be put to death. George begged him to spare their lives. Then George decided to spend *all* his time helping Christians, and gave up being a soldier. He was a brave follower of Christ.

This is a story which is told about brave George.

There was a lake in North Africa where a dragon lived. Every evening the dragon came out of the lake looking for its supper. Each day the poor people in the village near the lake brought two sheep to give to the dragon.

At last there were no sheep left. So the people drew lots to see who should be given to the dragon. The king's daughter was chosen.

The king offered money to the villagers to save his daughter ; but they would not take it. Many had given their children to the dragon.

While the princess was waiting by the lake, George came riding by. He asked her why she was crying, and the princess told him about the dragon.

"In the Name of Jesus I will kill the dragon," said George. "Do not be afraid."

When the dragon came out of the lake, brave George rode forward to fight and kill it. Soon the dragon was dead.

The king was so glad. He had a big church built, and he and his people became Christians. George had shewn them how faith in God and Jesus could help them overcome difficulties.

ST. ANDREW

The name Andrew is said to mean 'manly'.

Andrew was one of the first disciples to follow Jesus. Andrew had a brother named Simon Peter. They were both fishermen and sons of a fisherman named Jonas of Bethsaida in Galilee.

Andrew had heard from John the Baptist about Jesus coming to teach, and he was probably watching when Jesus was baptised by John. There were wonderful happenings when Jesus was baptised. God's Spirit, like a dove, descended upon Jesus, and a voice from Heaven said, "This is my beloved Son in whom I am well pleased."

The very first thing Andrew did after he had decided to follow Jesus, was to look for his brother, Simon Peter, and tell him all about Jesus.

Matthew, another disciple, describes how the brothers were busy in their fishing boat. The Lord Jesus called to them from the shore: "Follow Me, and I will make you fishers of men". By this He meant that he would make them into missionaries, and that they would tell other people of Christ's teachings.

Matthew tells us that the two brothers at once left their boat, and followed Jesus.

Saint Andrew later travelled about as a missionary, and many people learned to love God as a result of his work.

Andrew was put to death in Greece, on a cross shaped like a letter 'X', by those who did not believe his teaching. This Saint Andrew's cross is now part of our national flag, the Union Jack.

A legend gives the reason for his being the Patron Saint of Scotland: the story says that some relics, or bones, of the Saint were brought from Greece to Scotland by a priest named Regulus in the eighth century. The place where the relics were believed to be buried is now the town of St. Andrew's.

SAINT DAVID

David must have been a happy boy. The old stories tell us that in church he had a sweet singing voice. Most Welsh people love music, and can sing well.

Even when David was still a boy, people knew that he wanted to serve God in a special way when he grew up.

One of David's teachers was an old man named Paulinus. It was he who taught David about the Bible and helped him to understand its teachings.

One story tells us that when old Paulinus was going blind, David restored his sight by touching his eyes.

When David was older, he travelled about Wales preaching and teaching the people about God.

David was loved by everyone, especially those who served and worked in the monasteries he had built.

He planned gardens near the monasteries. Vegetables and herbs and flowers grew there. The wild leek, which is the emblem of Wales, perhaps grew in those gardens.

One of the best known monasteries is said to have been where the place called St. David's stands to-day. Here a fine old cathedral is named after him.

One day there was a big meeting in Wales. Thousands of people went to hear their Bishops speak to them about God.

The crowd was so big that no one could hear what the Bishops were saying. The wind blew the sound of their voices away. Old Paulinus was in the crowd, and he remembered his pupil, David.

"Let David speak. You will hear *his* voice," shouted Paulinus. So everyone called for David to come forward.

David first prayed to God for help, then he spoke clearly to the crowd about God and His love. *Everyone* heard his voice!

David later became Archbishop of South Wales.

SAINT PATRICK

Saint Patrick is the patron saint of Ireland. There are many tales told of the wonderful things Patrick did for Ireland.

No one is sure where he was born. Some writers think Scotland was the place. Like other boys, Patrick was more fond of adventure than of learning his lessons.

When he was about sixteen he was carried off by pirates to Ireland, and there sold as a slave with other boys. He looked after sheep and pigs for his master. It was a hard and lonely life for a boy like Patrick.

After seven years Patrick got away from Ireland. As he grew older he began to think how best he could return to Ireland.

He had a dream and heard a voice telling him that one day he must teach the Irish about God. First Patrick went to France and Italy to be trained as a priest. Later he was made a Bishop.

After a long time Patrick sailed back to Ireland to be the friend, teacher and Bishop of the Irish. He travelled all over Ireland teaching, building churches and helping people.

The people of Ireland loved to listen to St. Patrick telling them about God.

Here is part of Saint Patrick's beautiful hymn which is still sung to-day:

*I bind to myself this day
The power of God to guide me,
The might of God to uphold me,
The wisdom of God to teach me,
The eye of God to watch over me,
The ear of God to hear me,
The Word of God to give me
speech,
The hand of God to protect me,
The way of God to lie before me,
The shield of God to guard me.*

SAINT FRANCIS OF ASSISI

The father of Francis was a rich merchant who sold silk and cloth.

As a young man, Francis was very gay and happy, and enjoyed life with his friends. When he was older he became a soldier.

Later on, Francis left the army and decided to become a soldier of Jesus. He gave away his money, rich clothes and sword, and tried to be a good Christian, helping the sick and poor.

Some of his friends laughed at Francis for doing good, but others followed him and were glad to serve God and those in need.

Francis wore a coarse brown cloth robe, with a cord for a belt, and no shoes. He went about preaching and teaching about God and His Son, Jesus Christ.

When he had a number of good companions to help him, he sent them out, two by two, to do as he did, preaching and helping the sick and poor.

They had no money, but the people who listened to these Brothers, or Friars as they were later called, gave them food.

There were many stories written and told about Brother Francis, and the wonderful way he had with wild animals and birds. He loved all God's creatures.

One story about Francis tells how he met a boy carrying a basket of wild doves to sell in the market.

When Francis saw the doves imprisoned in the small basket, he felt very unhappy. He believed that we should never be unkind to birds or animals.

"Will you give those doves to me?" said Francis to the boy. When the basket was opened, the doves flew out and perched on the shoulder of kind Francis. They went with him along the road to the town.

Francis called the doves Little Sisters, and was happy that they were now free to live as God intended.

SAINT CHRISTOPHER

Many of the old stories about this saint tell us that he was very tall and strong. Because of his great strength, Christopher wanted to serve the most powerful king or master in the whole wide world.

But each time he found a king to work for, he also found that this new master knew of someone even more powerful. So Christopher went on with his search for work.

Then one day Christopher met a hermit, or holy man. He talked to Christopher about the Lord Jesus Christ, who was King of all heaven and earth.

"How may I serve the Lord Jesus," asked Christopher. The hermit told him to use his strength in helping others. This was how the greatest King of all wanted people to serve Him.

The holy man told Christopher about a river close to a church. The river was fast and deep and hard to cross. There was no bridge there.

"You could easily carry people across the river," said the hermit, "you are so strong. You would be serving Christ that way."

Then Christopher built a log hut so that he could live by the river.

Christopher carried people over the deep river in all kinds of weather. He used a strong tree branch as a staff to help him wade across.

The story tells us that one night a little child asked to be carried across the river. Christopher waded over bearing the child on his shoulders. When they reached the other side, the child told Christopher, "I am the Christ Child. Plant your staff in the earth. In the morning you will know that what I say is true."

Christopher did so. Next day his staff had grown beautiful, white flowers.

Christopher means 'Christ-bearer' or 'Christ-carrier.'

SAINT MARGARET
OF SCOTLAND

Saint Margaret was a real princess. She sailed from England to Scotland with her brother, Prince Edgar, and her sister, Princess Christina.

The journey by sea was long and stormy, but at last they reached harbour safely.

Malcolm, King of Scotland welcomed them and fell in love with the beautiful Princess Margaret. Later they were married, so Margaret became Queen Margaret.

Margaret wanted to serve God in a special way. She prayed that He would show her how best she could do this in her new homeland.

The King and Queen loved each other very much. A church was built in Dunfermline to show their thanks to God for such happiness.

They lived in the big grey castle in Edinburgh, and had a family of eight children. Queen Margaret read to them from her own precious books. In the castle was a little chapel, and each day she prayed there that God would help her to serve Him and the people of Scotland.

Everyone was happier because of the kindness of Queen Margaret. She had schools opened where children could learn to read and write.

The castle that had been so gloomy became a friendly and cheerful place. Queen Margaret showed mothers how to make gay clothes for their children, and how to weave bright materials.

Every day the castle doors were opened to the poor and sick and needy. Every day the Queen loved to feed little orphan children, and to mother them. She loved them all.

The people of Scotland loved good Queen Margaret. She did so much for them because of her love for God.

SAINT JOAN OF ARC

Joan, or Jeanne D'Arc was born on a farm in a French village called Domrémy.

Joan loved her home. Her mother taught her how to use the spinning wheel, and how to sew and help in the house. She also learned how to mind the sheep and cattle, and she cared for all creatures great and small.

Everyone in the village loved kind-hearted Joan. The other children in the village were her friends, and she ran about and played with them in the fields.

One day when Joan was alone in her father's field, she heard a heavenly voice telling her that she had been chosen to do brave deeds. The voice told her that she must fight and help the Dauphin Charles to be crowned King of France.

At first Joan was frightened. At that time she was only about thirteen years old, and she wondered how she could ever lead an army into battle. But she believed the voice, and she knew that it was God who wanted her to do this. So Joan did obey.

At first the Dauphin did not believe that Joan could help him. Then he gave her a suit of shining armour, a fine horse and a splendid banner.

Joan rode at the head of the army, cheering on the soldiers and making them brave like herself. Great battles were won, and the Dauphin was crowned King of France.

Much later on, Joan was captured and put to death by those who refused to believe that the voice had come to her from God. But all over the world she is now known as Saint Joan of Arc.

Series 606A